ONE WORD

ONE WORD

MARC J. STRAUS

TRIQUARTERLY BOOKS
NORTHWESTERN UNIVERSITY PRESS

Evanston, Illinois

TriQuarterly Books

Northwestern University Press

Evanston, Illinois 60208-4210

Second paperback printing 1997

Library of Congress Cataloging-in-Publication Data

Straus, Marc J.

One word / Marc J. Straus

p. cm.

"TriQuarterly books."

ISBN 0-8101-5010-7 (cloth).

—ISBN 0-8101-5035-2 (paper)

1. Medicine—Poetry. I. Title.

PS3569.T6921305   1994

811'.54—dc20   94-12816

CIP

Contents

3

4

Acknowledgments

Poems collected in this volume were first published in the following: *Akros Review*, "Reconciliation," "The X-ray Report"; *Black Warrior Review*, "The List," "Luck," "Neuroanatomy Summer"; *Field*, "An Elephant Crossed the Road"; *Greensboro Review*, "The Collector"; *Herman Review*, "Train Revelations"; *Journal of the American Medical Association*, "Autumn"; *Kenyon Review*, "Lecture to Third-Year Medical Students"; *Lullwater Review*, "Carotid Aneurysm," "My Inner Ear"; *Passages North*, "A Pause," "Hannibal in the Alps on a Sunday," "Informed Consent," "Marlene Dietrich's Dead," "My Seventh Birthday"; *Phoebe*, "Curiosity," "December 11th"; *Poetry East*, "Questions and Answers," "Pocket Calendar"; *Ploughshares*, "One Word," "What I Heard on the Radio Today"; *Snail's Pace*, "The Size of the Lesion," "Uncle Aaron Has Alzheimer's Disease"; *TriQuarterly*, "A Big Black Crow," "The Bogeymen," "Dr. Gold & Dr. Green," "Dr. Gold & Dr. Green, II," "Lecture to Second-Year Medical Students," "The Log of Pi," "St. Maarten Vacation"; *Western Journal of Medicine*, "People Who Live in Glass Houses," "Twelve Words."

"Scarlet Crown," "One Word," "The Size of the Lesion," "What I Heard on the Radio Today," "The Log of Pi," "Neuroanatomy Summer," "Lecture to Third-Year Medical Students," "The List," "A Pause," "Hannibal in the Alps on a Sunday," "An Elephant Crossed the Road," "Informed Consent," and "Autumn" appear in *Scarlet Crown* (Aureole Press, 1994).

ONE WORD

1

A Pause

What did the test show, his daughter asked.
There was this momentary pause, an amount
of time to delay still acceptable, maybe
one and a half seconds or so. That's the gap

in which I've no conscious thought. I don't
plan what I'll say, but it must be a time
these neurons need to dwell over the answer
internally. I see how the mouth is framed,

just the way the lips are left parted, how
the head is tilted slightly down and pupils
widen. I see her hands cupped around
the chair's arms, fingers pulled in tight,

feet pulled deep underneath.
Her pocketbook, large and full left
on an exam table, the X-ray envelope
nearby. She could see the name

on the cover, could see writing
if she wished, that said CT of brain.
But she doesn't look that way. She looks
hard at me while I pause ever so slightly.

The Log of Pi

I remember the log of Pi, the battle
of Antietam, the insertion of the biceps, the action
of Adriamycin. Why? When's the last time
anyone asked these data? I've filled my head

with assorted facts, ordered and chronoed,
sorted and cataloged. Maybe a game-show host
will choose me. I'll win stacks of money
answering questions about paramecia, Picasso's

pink period, the sequence of DNA, the dose
of 5FU. But no, they always ask the question
I never knew. They ask me over
and over again, every day. First

I pretend not to hear. Then I change
the subject. Then when pressed I say,
the answer floats on angel's lips
and is whispered in our ear just once.

Scarlet Crown

I met a man my age running a greenhouse.
He pointed to the pots with pride, saying
they contained a thousand separate cacti.
Not much interest in these when I started,
he said. He pointed to the barbed bristles

(glochids), the bearing cushions (areoles),
and the names of many of the 200 genera:
Brain, Button, Cow-tongue, Hot-dog, Lace,
Coral, and Silver-ball. In my work,
I said, I'm burdened with such straight-

forward terms: lung cancer, lymphoma,
breast cancer, leukemia. I'd love
to switch to: Pond-lily, Star,
or Scarlet Crown. Really, he said,
pointing to other plants, named

Hatchet, Devil, Dagger, Hook, and
Snake—or perhaps a diagnosis of this:
Rat-tail, White-chin, Wooly-torch,
or Dancing-bones.

The Size of the Lesion

"Almost time now," he said. For what,
I wondered, knowing I wouldn't ask,
some things better left unsaid, or leaving
the possibility of a different

interpretation. It's this way more
as time goes on. A daughter comes in late
and you don't say exactly what you feel
and her vague answer is probably

all you want to hear. Patients are proficient
at this. You tell them the X ray showed
little change, knowing they won't ask
if the lesion's a little smaller or larger.

Dr. Gold & Dr. Green

You know, when I first became ill
I went to see that pill
Dr. Gold. He'd never smile

like you. He'd come in with a long face
being evas-
ive, always staring at his shoelaces.

I know I shouldn't say that to you,
but what can I do?
I never knew

what was going on. I was ready to quit,
and then you'd come in and sit
here and make me feel it

was worth it, the pain and nausea,
the awful mouth sores and diarrhea,
and those low counts and fever.

I always say God bless you Dr. Green.
Dr. Gold has track shoes on. You never seem
to be in a hurry even

though you're so busy. I trust
you, but you know how nervous
I get when you tell us

the results of the tests.
I know I can be such a pest,
but I'd like a little rest

before the next treatment, at least till
I'm stronger. You know I'm responsible
and I'll come in when I'm not this ill.

Twelve Words

I even dream of calling you,
to discuss my options, as it were,

to ask if the pain in the shoulder
is related to the mass in the neck

which seems less swollen, even though
it occurred just after the drugs

which may have caused the nausea
and certainly precipitated the weight loss

(not that I had any leeway),
unlike the hair loss, which I agree

is merely vanity in a man my age,
but it focused on the tracheostomy

which I press with my thumb to speak, but
I'm never understood, and yet

only you come by and talk to me
without shouting as others do,

suggesting that I am also deaf
(which I am certainly not),

so that I must respond by writing
on this yellow pad in bold script

knowing that your time is valuable
needing to see many people,

so I have promised to limit myself
to twelve words each day.

Dr. Gold & Dr. Green, II

Eleanor, did you mean
that I'm Dr. Gold or Dr. Green?
It certainly seemed

that when you described
how Dr. Green always tried
to spend time with you, it applied

to me. I thought I did my best
to review the results of the tests
with you, knowing how depressed

you were. I was cautious to avoid the one word
that would always perturb
you. I heard

the pain pressing on your trachea
and saw the waves of nausea,
the mouth sores and bouts of diarrhea.

But some days I suppose
I too had track shoes on. Were those
the days you chose

to call me Dr. Gold?
Now, I only wish you had told
me how impersonal, how controlled

I was. I guess there were times, dear Eleanor,
that I was simply unable to do more.
I didn't recognize this before

your poem "Dr. Gold and Dr. Green." You tried
to say that each of us has two sides.
I wish I understood this before you died.

Autumn

Sometimes you say it's smaller. Today
you say there's little difference compared
to last week, and last week, I remember
you said it was a touch larger, and you'd change

the treatment. Yesterday there was a toad
outside my window after the rainstorm.
The season for flies was over and its song
was decadent. The apples have reddened

and the crabgrass has died leaving
a perfect lawn. In the early morning
the tips of the leaves have a silver
sheen. The lake behind O'Dywer's house

has those coruscating ripples at 7 A.M.
Brandon's dog is barking. The yellow school bus
pops out the stop sign and four kids climb
inside. A little one looks back. His mother's

rubbing her hands together thinking about
the day's errands. Her husband will be home
on the 6:54, open the door, lay down
his paper and fix a drink. I would touch

the lump myself to be certain
but it's already chilly out. I'll order
some logs and lay in a good supply
for winter, wondering what you'll say next week.

Hannibal in the Alps on a Sunday

It was Sunday. I remember that
now. I wasn't working, but beginning
to think about working, thinking about

exercising which I hadn't done
in weeks. You had said keep up
the exercise. Try to stay fit, and

maintain your weight. Under the circumstances
these seemed mutually exclusive. Somewhere,
walking outside, looking at the last

of the daisies, at the remnants
of a half-hearted garden, I knew
the swelling was back. It was a subtle

recognition. Maybe when bending over
some sense of my anatomy after 42 years
was changed, a hint of an intruder

as my arm swung back to my side, a soft
impediment. What will you tell me
this time, the third time? You will have

certain plans for me, making the journey sound
effortless. You could have planned
Hannibal's march over the mountains

with ease, with a smile and a firm grip.
But what if on some Sunday it snowed
again in the Alps and he used up

all the oxen pulling the carts this far? And
what if the food gave out and the path was covered
with snow? What would you say that Sunday?

Luck

Just my luck. I gave up smoking last month
and the doctor says there's a lesion in my lung.

If I'm lucky, he says, it'll be curable.
I tell him the TV showed two kids rescued

from a burning building and the reporter said
it's lucky they're alive. So I say, how come

it's lucky they got second degree burns. How come
they were in the building in the first place.

Want to hear about real luck, I say. I have this itch
under my arm. I'll scratch it twice in slow circles

and the lesion in my lung is gone.

Reward

I used to think that way,
to believe there was reward
for good deeds. Yet even
as a youngster I was warned
the rewards weren't obvious,
or were deferred to the hereafter.

Some people never wonder
what they'll say when told
the end is near. They don't say
"why me?" When told they've
a few years left they're consoled.
I prefer not knowing. It sufficed

to know everyone died sooner or later.
The "later" was consolation.
If you say this disease was there
for years that's no consolation
since now I know, and
knowing's no reward.

Questions and Answers

"Why complain," the old Jew
always says. The Irish man
says nothing. The black man
seeded with pain from the prostate

tumor withholds, says less
than is so—until that day,
maybe after you've held his arm,
touched him gently, that he'll look

at your white face, and ask
a question. The question
might be so simple, so clear
that you're unprepared to answer.

$\overline{2}$

Lecture to Second-Year Medical Students

(for Peter Russo)

This morning I'd like to concentrate
on the case of a 28-

year-old man with non-Hodgkin's lymphoma
treated with the COMLA

regimen,
an acronym

for the 5 drugs given intravenously,
simultaneously

with radiation. Cytoxan cleaves the DNA
similarly to high intensity radia-

tion. In fact, the dosage 50 miles from Chernobyl
produced a fraction of the cell kill

he received in 10 seconds. It produces nausea
in 1 hour, diarrhea

in 1 day, leukopenia and anemia in 1 week, and hair loss
in 1 month. Of course

the goal is to kill the vagrant
cancer cells with errant

DNA. If we calculate the ratio
of cells killed (normal versus cancer), we know

the odds of response
for each level of toxicity. Once

we establish his specific tolerance
it's possible to balance

competing factors. Then we determine
the interim

blood counts, and retreat
as soon as recovery is almost complete.

Oncovin causes neurological toxicity
with high specificity

for the hands and feet. Whenever
these drugs are given together

loss of libido and impotence are common. Methotrexate
causes mouth sores and interferes with folate

metabolism. The Leukovorin acts as an antidote
which is started about

6 hours later. Adriamycin
often causes dose-dependent cardiac damage within

9 to 12 months and therefore
it's essential to monitor

cardiac output. The complete response rate
is 80% and the cure rate

is at least 30%, provided that a full dose
of each drug is given. For those

patients who fail initial therapy,
as he did, response to further chemotherapy

is marginal. The data suggest
that survival is only limited at best,

because, as the pharmacologic
resistance increases the therapeutic

index is reduced. Side effects continually increase
while the chances of success inevitably decrease.

One must weigh
the risk-versus-benefit ratio and convey

this information accurately to the patient.
In this man I'd recommend further experimental treatment.

What I Heard on the Radio Today

Horowitz debuted a Schumann piece
in 1928. This new recording
is acoustically precise, with
a persistent cough from the audience,

loud, in two parts, both exhaled sounds,
(B-flat, then C-sharp) the second
higher and more forceful. It sounds like
a man's cough, a mature man,

in his forties or fifties. You can tell these things
just as you can guess gender and age
from a voice on the phone. This man coughing,
not covering his mouth, no handkerchief muffle,

may have served in World War I. He would have been
of moderate rank, a sergeant in charge
of a platoon. He took orders
and gave orders. He may have worked

in an insurance firm, and sold policies
to pensioners. Now V. P.
and three kids in school, life was bright.
Coolidge was President. He had $42,000

in assorted stocks. And Horowitz,
Horowitz was a skinny Jew from Russia
who could play piano, but Jews
were good at things like that. Russia

and Poland knew how to treat their Jews.
And here at Carnegie Hall, at four dollars
a ticket, he played Schumann
with such intended panache. The cough

continued as the concert went on.
I know that cough. I've heard it
listening to many lungs
on TB wards. It has its own pattern

and tone. His cough worsened in a year
when the market crashed. His breath
became more shallow. His stocks
were worthless. His daughter married a Jew.

Late, much too late, he'd be moved to
a sanitorium and die in '32.
There remains a recording of him
that I heard on the radio today.

St. Maarten Vacation

1. ON THE PLANE

Winter lunges in before I leave.
On the plane I already
smell the breeze and hear
the gull's *cacoo*. The sun
darts through the fractured leaves.
Who will manipulate
Larry's dose of 5FU? Who will know
every value
and push the chemo, wishing,
wishing the lesion away?

2. THE CHAIR BOYS

They put out chairs each day
by the water,
two in a row, in the best location
for the right tip. No shady spot
for me
fair skinned and freckled. I came
too late
and didn't have
two bits. That's my history,

needing shade and sunscreen
on a Caribbean beach. When I go
to heaven
I won't need shade

or a hat. The chair boys
will be lined up in two rows
allowing only redheads
to pass through.

3. THE YELLOW BATHING SUIT

The girl in the yellow
bathing suit—a perfect
body. She lost her virginity
last year. Next year she'll be
in college getting A's and B's.
In twelve years her
husband will leave for the
girl in the red suit.

4. CUTTY SARK AT MULLET BAY

Amber in cold glass, four dollars
an ounce. A Catholic from Donegal
opened the spout
and pressed it
on its way. A Creole trucked it.
A Jamaican stacked it.
A Dutchman sold me
half a glass and charged it
to my room. I poured it
on the sand
which jaundiced
like my Polish
father's eyes.

5. EILEEN

A sixteen-year-old girl
is slapped by her mother
across the mouth
for dropping a book
in the sand.

Oh, Eileen. I will dream
it never happened. I will dream
her arm broke off,
that I intervened for you
as no one did
for me.

6. A RUSTY NAIL AT MULLET BAY

They sidle up to the bar in briefs
and bikinis and ask
for this improbable drink. An
oxymoron. What's in it? Metal,
tetanus? They drink two
and push the stock market away.

The Ray-Bans are on. The laugh
is real. A good tan, a new face
appears from Englewood,
and they order a third.

7. DYED HAIR

This vacation went so fast,
mornings by the beach, afternoons
diving to sixty feet, and nights
in a French café. I saw
an old man with dyed hair
alone on a beach chair.
That will be me
in a blink.

8. THE MILKY WAY

Back on the overbooked plane,
the lady insisted on smoking. "Go ahead,"
I said. I'd had
my week on the beach—clean air,
crystal sky. I'd stared at night
to count the stars. The Milky Way
had fluffy lights
and smoky edges,
just like
lung cancers I see
on X-ray films.

Time

So here I am, and now you'll be telling me
you told me so till eternity. Anyway, Sam,
when my son gives a speech today, as I gave yours

six years ago, we'll see who mourns for me,
who cries, and for how long. Which leads me to ask
about time. I always imagined that heaven meant

having perfect time. In life we rush incessantly
and lament how fast it passes. Now, I hope that time
can be compressed as tight as atomic rings,

so you wouldn't grieve or wait in pain. Or, time
is as expansive as photons splaying the universe,
so sadness is stalled. Time would be an accordion

making music, opening and closing. I always wondered
how you waited on the hard table as we twirled
the tiny tube into a bleeding artery. I wondered why

you took this journey, fearless, telling me
with your index finger that I tried, the finger
that showed me how sheets were stacked, towels sold,

in your store, on Grand Street, where I learned to grow.
I pushed the chemo and washed your back until you said
that time is yours, not mine. I wished otherwise. Now,

your black eyes burn my face, hold my aching legs in place.
The ground is reaching up to touch my soles, and some hand
is pressing my back. Why? Tell me before you fade

into a million molecules. Tell me everything quickly
while I'm losing you. Tell me about time again.
Point at me with your finger that I miss.

Curiosity

Can someone be so curious that they would put their nose
over a beaker of sulfuric acid? Would they touch a boiling pot
on the stove? Even my dog doesn't lick hot meat. It's simple

enough to smell the container when you remove it from the
    fridge.
Simple enough to put a thermometer in the pot or in a mouth.
Would you call a doctor if your baby was running a hundred and
    four

or would you wait to see if blisters break out? Would you walk
in Watts in a three-piece suit at midnight, you idiot?
You might as well jump out of a plane without checking

the chute. You might as well put a blinking light on your head
and walk back into the old ghetto in Poland. Tell them
only you survived and they're all dogs. Worse yet, stupid dogs.

Tell them their mouths are screwed down at the corners
from years of grimacing in malice. Tell the Ukraine marching
on the corner that he's a killer too. Tell the proselytizer selling

"Jews For Jesus" that his mother cries in her grave. You did all
    that.
And yet, on August fifth you said you were curious and unafraid.
I said what if there's no discovery, or worse,

what if it's the beginning of interminable hardship. You said
you wondered about this for years, wondered why everyone is
    afraid
of something inevitable. I said it pays to wait, pays

to try new treatment. You said you were curious and had waited
long enough.

The Bogeymen

Sometimes the sound of violence is so soft
it barely tips the antennae of a summer's
moth. There's a pattern to its thud
that mixes neatly with coffee machines
and children's laughter. Then, at that moment
of conscious recognition we know the tune
is old and familiar—and we avoided it,
did we not? A certain quiet, a lost
adjective, an eyelash an angstrom off.

Sometimes the silence is hidden in the eyes,
a tiny blepharospasm that we physicians see.
And yet, it eluded me for twenty-three years. I remember
how she hid behind the screen, as I intervened
when the fury focused at her. I'd protected my sister
from the bogeymen, real and imagined.
Why did she endure this indignity alone
while I shed the ghosts of my scars?

We're told that we get used to things,
like the noise of the subway rattling by
or the wash on the neighbor's line, the first
gray hair, and the second. The first
lost hair. What choice do we have?
We can choose not to smoke. We can choose
to move. We can put up our hand and say,
"silence is only broken by clarity,
and by me."

Uncle Aaron Has Alzheimer's Disease

His son asks what he had for breakfast
and a helium balloon, oblong and silver
floats above the maple tree. Grandpa Max says

they're like birds set free. The aide wedges meat
between his teeth and green pea soup dribbles
down his cheek. I'll eat those eggs, he says,

if I can swallow them raw. His leg swings off
the chair and jams against the door. Frankie
Johnson's yelling that Jews are chickenshits.

He hits Frankie in the face with both fists
as the orderly grabs restraints. The nurse bends
to hold him down and Ann Cohen's breast touches his arm,

so he squeezes it. The TV's on. Abbott's slapping
Costello, Milton's dressed in drag, and Groucho's giving
away one hundred dollars for saying the lucky word.

An Elephant Crossed the Road

An elephant crossed the road and everyone
    bowed to the ground.
He couldn't play the piano. I told
    you that.
Worms came out only on dry days. A Copt
    hummed a verse.
Ten yards of cotton cut to the match. Two pairs
    of pinch-pleated drapes.
Rivers drowned in each other's mouths, and
    blisters were everywhere.
I saw the scar where the dog bit him
    when he was seven.
Lesions were so deep they broke
    the bone.
He rubbed the cloth between two fingers,
    just as I'm doing now.

There were two lines and a lonely man
    waved a wand back and forth.
He bought me two hot dogs so I'd leave
    the game early.
The man who played the violin got one potato. The other
    got none.
His stepmother took his soup away
    and gave it to the fat boy.
A boy stood in the distant doorway with an apple
    in his hand.

He went to the suburb where
    they judge your lawn.
There were no tattoo parlors, but everyone
    had one.
He had silk shirts and wide ties
    before it was fashionable.

The skin was so thin a light could shine
    through.
He learned a new word every day. Imagine
    his vocabulary when he was forty.
Shoes were left before the gate, a disposal
    problem of major proportion.
He bought so many shoes, that even now,
    many remain in unopened boxes.
An elf walked onto a plank and said,
    "it's a shorter jump for me."
He said that 90-inch drapes were 89 inches long.
    That one inch made America rich.
The smell wrapped round the universe, as Churchill
    and Roosevelt puffed cigars.
A bedspread named for a president sold
    for sixteen-fifty.

The smoke was the color of cream, beautiful,
    costly, facial cream.
He bought six pairs of identical sneakers
    for two dollars a piece.
A man stood up and discussed Voltaire while
    two corpses clapped out loud.

He bought a Cadillac. He said
he got a good deal.

A man traded a Fabergé egg for an
orange. The orange was stale.

He sold our home to a guy on the train. It became
quite valuable later on.

Centipedes had an extra leg, and the yard
was full of unborn children.

He hated cats. I always thought
mine ran away.

A crocus was lit by the moonlight and a fly flew
over the universe between two eyebrows.

When I was 15 I met a 25-year-old with half a brain.
They left in the part that forgives.

The casket was the size of the ancient temple
and people lay in layers.

When he wouldn't pay me enough I sold 300
dictionaries.

There were 12 apostles, 3 wise men, 1 virgin
and only 1 Jew. Judas.

He bought Penn Central for six, and sold
at three.

Three fish swam in a school. That's all
that was left.

Did you know he shortened his name by one syllable
the year I was born?

Crickets chirped one at a time. One
at a time. One at a time.

A pancreas cancer starts with one cell
  which refuses to die.
Kierkegaard, Nietzsche, Wagner—blame them,
  they're all dead.
I worked in our textile store once a week
  until I finished medical school.
Questions were posed after the facts, and the facts
  were altered every day.
I never questioned why I went into oncology
  until that day.
A child asks four questions on Passover. It takes
  3000 years to answer.
You asked me why I treated him.
  Don't ask!

The Passover story is backwards. The angel
  of death smote the Almighty.
When I said it was pancreas cancer his silence
  filled our mouths to the brim.
The philosopher asked about the noise a falling tree makes
  in the forest. Who cares?
There's a sign on the corner of Grand and Eldridge
  with his name.
The town of Sambor used to be in Poland. Now it's
  only in my memory.
His obituary was in the New York Times,
  of course.
The ground is filled with a million moles who'll all
  come out on Groundhog Day.
Put it this way, am I supposed to only
  care for strangers?

Marlene Dietrich's Dead

I've always supposed she had Nazi leanings
based on her movie roles, but the *Times* says
it wasn't so; she was a heroine.
At the NIH, a patient, Charlie Plott
(I'm sure it's okay to use his name now),

allowed me to sample his cancer
every hour for several days. I learned
how lung cancer grows and which cells respond
to chemo. After I published this data
I heard that Charlie had transferred to us

from death row. Recently, a Polish realtor
showed me a house. He claimed he was in
the underground, and a German prisoner
of war. When the Jews marched three miles
from Auschwitz to Birkenau,

to the ovens, the people along the way
say they never knew what happened.
They only saw thin people, dressed
in striped clothes. Some noticed
that the marchers always went one way.

Hand Prayer

I saw a ceremony once where a priest
laid his hands on the baby's head, and another

where the rabbi touched its temples. In my home
my grandmother covered her eyes when saying

the starting Sabbath prayer. Now my wife,
now my daughter do the same. No one ever

said how these uses of hands came about.
When I was in medical school I learned

to tap the chest, to press for livers
and spleens, to feel for lumps in breasts.

Oh God, give us hands that signal the genesis
of life, the permanence of tradition.

3

A Big Black Crow

My portion is small. A couple
of worms. Some maggots. Nothing
that would interest you. I sat
on this old carcass once, on a quiet
highway, hardly having to move all day
for twelve wheelers. I almost
fell asleep and some kid pulls up on a bike
and watches me. I watch him. He's
too young to be disgusted, not
tainted yet by adults pouring
cream in coffee, dipping meats
in alcohol, frying perfectly fresh food
until it drips like sap
from an old maple, licking hot fat
off their lips. So I stare
at him, nice kid with red hair
and brown eyes, as if to say,
I cherish my portion. It's small.
A maggot here. A maggot there.

The Rabbit Field

(Sambor, Poland)

They came to the rabbit field
in white shorts and tennis shoes,
a field the rabbits staked out
years ago. The rabbits—

white-tailed, gray,
were spread out, dozens
standing calmly
in lush grass, some darting

in and out of brush. Then
a leader in a bathrobe
and brown boots raised
his right arm shoulder high, fingers

tight, and all the others did
the same. The rabbit field was set
ablaze, the warrens ransacked,
the objects of their devotion placed

in piles and burned. A photo
of one rabbit was found
with a face
much like mine.

My Seventh Birthday

I was told not to touch the Torah;
it was holy. Read it with a silver pointer
the cantor said. Each handwritten letter
must be perfect or the scroll cannot

be used. It takes a year, he said,
for the scribe to finish a single Torah.
Our synagogue has seven, I said, that's seven
years of work, as many years as me.

That's why they're so costly, he said.
Why did the Nazis burn them? I asked.
Surely there would always be others.
They wanted to destroy one year

of a Jewish life with each Torah burned,
he said. And if they burned these seven
would that be like burning me? I asked.
No, he said, you can always write another.

Uncle Hy's Package

If I could come visit you more often
maybe you'll tell me about your parents,
I said. What for, Grandma Katy said.

Let the dead lie dead. What were they like?
Did your mother teach you to cook? At this
she smiled and put out the home-baked

bread, stuffed kishka, and soup. I walked
to 51st Street to her apartment, up the tall
stoop and the stairs to the second floor.

I'll come visit you every week, I said,
if you tell me what Uncle Hy did in the war.
I sent him salamis hidden in bread, she said.

The Arcade

The end of a useless winter day,
and an hour to catch a train to Chappaqua,
I crossed the corner at 47th Street
and entered a long arcade: French scarves,
Italian ties, British coats, Taiwan toys.
The other end was quiet and I'm thinking,
not even the banks are ours.

Looking down I see my newly polished shoes
sinking in white hot sand which stretches forward
in ripples past palm trees to turquoise water
lapping easily against it, people swimming
or strolling on the beach, women topless,
one with dark nipples nearly brushing
my three-piece suit, smiling at me.

Maybe I'll take a quick swim, I think,
looking for the lockers. Then remembering
I have no towel I turn back into the arcade.
Stores were closing quickly. Hand-held video games
seemed to be the rage, all of them contests
of destruction, one thing devouring another.
I'll buy one when I have more time, I think.

Pocket Calendar

Perhaps in the closet, in a jacket—I panic
when it's lost. Only four bucks
and I entrust it with the entire truth,

some notes, my schedule for months to come,
as if it guarantees I'll be on time,
not overlap important meetings. Sometimes

in the car, sometimes beneath some papers
on my desk it always finds a hideout.
At year end I'll switch it for the next one,

this one filed away in case I need to know
what I did on a specific day, a specific time.
But I never look again. The only things that count

are the things I've yet to do. This calendar,
pressing against my chest, is proof
that I'll do them, that there's time left for me.

The Collector

When you don't like yourself
you can always buy a gun. They're easy
to get in the U.S. A good pistol
is four hundred bucks, but you don't need

anything more than a $200 model.
But you won't want to miss or misfire,
and since you're brought up enjoying things
of quality, you'll probably spend

a thousand once you've compared them.
You'll check the action, the mechanism,
reliability, and then, being a collector,
you'll want another, far more precious.

cast about for a way to explain
his inertia. When I'd complain

that his work was slow,
that his experimental notebooks were below

par, he was sullen.
He never offered an opinion

or even a response. What are your goals?
I asked. Do you have a role

model? Finally in an exasperated tone
he said, you Americans have grown

up on cowboys
and indians. Your culture preaches freedom but destroys

individuality. Everyone must succeed
by a certain age. You weed

out the inept, the infirm, the poor, the old,
and everyone is controlled

by TV.
I envy

only your commercials. Why, Sokolow?
I asked. Why not our scientific know-

how, our farms or freedom to vote?
No, your commercials, he said. When a society can devote

such effort to choosing between Coke
and Pepsi, when it can joke

about constipation or which beer
causes virility, it's clear

it has great power. Why not great freedom,
Sokolow? Freedom, he said, is seldom

found and seldom understood.
Freedom is an illusion which would

vanish but for this consummate ego.
I, Sokolow,

have abandoned my imperious ego
and therefore, my work goes a little slow.

Train Revelations

The sign says, *in an emergency*
open this panel by turning ring fastener
and follow the instructions inside.
But what if the train's on fire and the panel's hot?
What if the train derails the way it did near Baltimore
and turns on its side? Then we'd fall down

and the panel would be on the ground
(and I couldn't crawl through it even if I could open it) or,
it would be on the ceiling some 12 feet away. I'd have to hoist
    myself up,
locking my legs into the seat rails, reaching up, with smoke
    and panic
all around and maybe some people bleeding
or unconscious. I'd try to twist the ring the right way
and the panel might pop out and smash my head. Chances are
    50/50
I'd be turned the wrong way so I'd have to twist my head
    90 degrees
to read inside. What would it say?

What words are hidden? Who has seen them?
I sense that if I read them a great secret will be revealed.
I would have opened Tutankhamen's crypt. The ark
at Ararat. And the words—the words put down
by an unknown railroad clerk perhaps in Lexington, Kentucky
would be revealed, the words of Martha,

Calvin, Molly, revealed to me. I would read it, read the ten lines
emblazoned on the tablets, read the note in the bottle
put out to sea. But just then the doors would fly open
and a fireman would yell in to exit. I would be pulled away,

coughing, cyanotic, hands singed, reaching back,
reaching to see the words put there for me.

Reconciliation

If I cough will you listen to my chest
and tell me if there's a frog inside, or a dime
or the edge of a peacock's feather that floated
across the pond the time we went out

in a rowboat, and, didn't you say
that things can always be fixed
except for the persistence of time,
which suppresses memories—
even good ones—even mine?

An anonymous note left on my desk said,
Never Forget! You said I'd forget
how you leaned against me as we danced

to Nat King Cole. You said I'd forget the blue plaid dress.
The Catcher in The Rye. The science teacher
who made you cry. December 11th. I said

God was a cultural crutch, Nixon and Kennedy
were alter evils, fairy tales were cruel
inventions of adults. You said I was too logical—

unemotional. That was thirty years ago. Now I know
when lumps are benign and lesions grow. I know
the leaves turn green on Thursdays. I was seven once

and I laughed at dogs humping in the street,
at a boy's tongue flicking a girl's ear. I say—
Mary's no virgin and God is breath. God's the feeling

in fingers, the hair on the back of the hand.
God's an old man mumbling from storage deep within.
God's a grandfather I never knew, a grandfather's fat

squeezing me when I was three. You'd say it's illogical—
impossible. I say I know this because
I knew you. I never forget.

The White Fedora

So say I come by wearing a white fedora
and a Gucci tie, with a thirty-thousand-dollar
diamond set in a platinum brooch from Cremona,

(we visited their violin museum), and say
I ask for one dance then and there to Mae
Walters and Johnnie Mathis on a 78, just the way

I did in Rachel Taylor's basement, and say when
you press against me I feel your beat, then
I touch the right side of your neck and lean

my head against your chin and shoulder,
and I bring you Jacaranda roses from Brazil, or
dates from Haifa which we visited just after

Florence where we got that locket from a vendor
outside the Uffizi, just a year before
one baby, two years before a second, and twenty-five before

you gave me the white fedora.

4

One Word

A man at the bus stop stooped
to retrieve a dime rolling toward
the drain. Looking at me, he said,
"No ordinary dime, mister." "Really?" I said,

thinking how life is sometimes reduced
to a single word, a reflex, a courtesy.
Like the time I interviewed this young man
for a job in my lab, my mind wandering,

not attached to the conversation,
at best noticing his outdated tie.
Perhaps in response to some statement,
I said, "Why?" Then sensing the opportunity

he answered more eloquently and that changed
everything. Like the time a woman walked
into my medical office for one thing
and I put my fingers in the crevice of her neck,

the right side, and touched a fullness
deep within, and I knew that moment
I would say one word to her and nothing
would ever be the same again.

Lecture to Third-Year Medical Students

(for Peter Russo)

My first recommendation—suction an ample
volume of bone marrow, separate a sample

for pathology, incubate the rest in fetal
media, freeze it, administer a lethal

dose of chemo, and then reinfuse
the marrow as soon as the white count is reduced

below 1,000. If the extracted marrow
is first allowed

to incubate with several newer monoclonal antibodies
residual cancer cells are killed, and metastases

are less likely. A frequent
problem in these young patients

is the development of resistance
which is related to the presence

of the C-Ras gene even
when

treatments have initially
been effective, especially

in highly aggressive lymphomas such as this.
There's very little chance that his

tumor will respond to such drastic treatment,
and indeed the mortality from marrow replacement

exceeds the cure rate. However, in my opinion
there's no other option.

Neuroanatomy Summer

The even flow of neuronal pattern was visible
on the green screen, as tiny electrodes were placed
directly into portions of the cat's brain.

I was given the job of sectioning incremental portions
of the brain and measuring the cat's response,
reflexes, gait, etc., until it became

decerebrate, that is, had no higher brain function
at all. Then the cat was rigid, fully stretched out
and unresponsive. What was remarkable, the professor

said, was that I had been able to take this cat
through twelve stepwise operations (surely the basis
of a paper) and keep the cat intact.

Later on I saw a man stretched out like that
and rigid with tubes in his nose and penis. Someone
more important than me was writing a paper, I thought.

Carotid Aneurysm

No way. No way, he yelled,
coughing on the last word, yellow

sputum running down his lip.
He was like this when he exhausted

himself in certainty.
    Once Sally said

that salads have plenty Vitamin C.
No way, he yelled three times.

Someone listening wouldn't know
he objected to the word "plenty."

(He admired Linus Pauling
to say the least.)

    His granddaughter
answered a question from a puzzle

out loud. No way, he yelled
and was right of course.

    After the stroke
the doctor told him he had aphasia,

but could still understand everything.
    No way. No way, he yelled.

An old man sitting up front in a hard chair, in a tattered
blue robe,
with legs crossed, was asked by the psychiatry resident,
"Do you know what to kill two birds with one stone means?"

Certainly, he said. If you were walking next to me
on 42nd Street
and a hoodlum ran by to steal your wallet he could put a knife
in your ribs,
and twist it until the blade broke off and you could fall on me,
your blood
pouring in my mouth, suffocating me, the collar of your coat
stretched
across my neck, and what good would it do to yell,
I've been here

before, it's not a memory lapse. I could tell you what
Jimmy Walker said
when he was mayor and you'd wonder if I made it up or why
they put me here
when I was twenty-five. But that was the beginning
of the Depression.
It was possible to stay awhile, avoid the bread lines and when
it was over
why go to World War II when here there was three squares
and a bed,
and after that the outside seemed bleak; people never realize it
when young like you. So you sit there casually, but nervous,

stethoscope showing from a side pocket, asking me
in front of sixty students this question, hoping I give you
a concrete rather than abstract answer. There are no metaphors

here. There are the same hallways, the same room,
same robe every day. But while I think about it,
what does it mean to you, people who live
in glass houses shouldn't throw stones?

Angiogenesis Factor

How did this happen, they always
ask. Some day I'm going to say, it starts
as a mutation, a deletion at chromosome
nineteen, inherited no doubt—that
tumor promoters, carcinogens, transform

the cells over twenty years. First
dysplastic, then neoplastic. That
angiogenesis factor augments metastasis
elsewhere, and . . . By now they look at me

limp-lipped numb. And that took
six years to learn, to assimilate,
I want to add, and all you want to hear
is—I don't know. No one knows
how this happens.

The List

Let me check my list, he said,
interrupting again, just as I was telling
his wife the treatment causes

hair loss. He was looking at her
in that unconscious way, thinking about her
bald, struggling to say, you can buy

a great wig. It's only temporary.
You'll still be beautiful. But the image
in his head was the time he met her,

age nineteen. Maybe it was the hair
he fell in love with first, long, thick
and brown with reddish glints. He wanted

to spread his fingers through it, pull her
to him. He'd washed her hair a thousand times,
he thought, looking at his list.

My Inner Ear

Can you give me an ear, she said,
not literally of course, asking me
once again to pay attention. I'd been thinking
about Horace, the way he threw up

the other day, long after his food was gone,
how he said it wasn't as bad
as the last time. He'd have fever
in a week and the chills would begin

and the antibiotics would make him ill.
The antinauseants would make him shake
and we'd have to change them, and then
he'd vomit again. What did the X ray show

he'd want to know, now six weeks after
the treatment began. He'd hope the effort
was worth it, but he wouldn't ask. I'd have
to hear his question with my inner ear.

Informed Consent

I wouldn't care if you had only told me,
he said, not saying what I didn't say.
Sometimes they say this after the fact,
after something rare occurs that's best

not mentioned in advance. For instance,
I say that the treatment often causes
hair loss and nausea, that the white count
may drop, leading to infection and sepsis,

that mouth sores are common, and bleeding
is possible. I say that the chances of cure
are slim, and improvement may not be seen
for months. Once, after the second course,

a small rash occurred, which faded
in three days. I said I didn't know
what caused it. He said I should have warned him
of this side effect in advance.

The X-ray Report

Sometimes, he said, I wake up imagining
that I didn't wake up, imagining if I did wake up
you'd be here with reports of X rays I haven't taken yet.

I live between reports, not the taking of tests
because they don't matter. When I lie in the machine
a computer measures my insides, but what matters

is what someone dictates. No, what really matters, he said,
(pointing at me), is what you say they said, not the archive
somewhere that is testimony that a test was done, which doesn't

measure my will or my spirit or what used to be before someone
insisted that this is reality, or what might be
if you or I decided to wake up.

Say Ninety-Nine

Say ninety-nine, the professor said, placing
the stethoscope to the patient's chest, facing
him away from us, six intense
twenty-two-year-olds. You'll hear the presence
of a high-pitched wheeze
audibly increased as the airways are squeezed
by the confluence of thousands of nodules
formed by exposure to silicon particles.

This forty-nine-
year-old man has undoubtedly worked in a mine
over twenty years. His chest is barrelled out
and no doubt
he's extremely short of breath, suggesting that before
long he'll require a tank. Also don't ignore
the size . . .

I caught a glimpse of him in the mirror: frog eyes,
frozen wide.

A Minor Issue

It's a minor issue. I thought
not to mention it, especially since these symptoms
have been transient. I mean, compared
to some of the problems you see

this is incidental. I came to you
recommended by John Butler. I'm sure
you remember John. He had a terrible
case of prostate cancer. You know,

spread all over, into the bones, not much
anyone could do, in a lot of pain.
Poor guy, knew him over thirty years.
I never came here with him, though

I drove him to the lab once. The guy
was a horse and then at the end
he was so thin, sitting like a stick
in his big chair, hardly able to move.

I'm sure you see this a lot, but it's
kind of a shock to see such deterioration
so rapidly. My mother died of old age,
the way it should be, just pooped out

after a full life, no prostate problems,
ha-ha, though I remember years ago she had
these fibroids which bled like crazy, had
a hysterectomy, but what the hell

it wasn't the big C, nothing that spread.
Like I said, I put off coming here
because it comes and goes and probably
isn't much of anything. Don't you agree?

Spawning Season

So you're saying it could go either way, he said
to me. But what are the odds, the toxicity?
What if I say no, let nature take

its course? . . . Once, when I was a boy
I lived by a river where the salmon spawned
each year. We created steps to ease their way

upstream, and here and there we also set traps
to catch a year's supply. Each fish filled
with roe jumped the steps or landed in nets.

When a pregnant salmon set out, she didn't
concern herself with the odds, the number of traps,
and there was no one present to explain them to her.

Lecture to Graduating Medical Students

(for Peter Russo, age 30)

In your second year I reviewed the case of P. R.,
a 28-year-old male who presented with far

advanced non-Hodgkins lymphoma
treated with the COMLA

regimen. He first achieved a complete
response and more intensive chemo was repeated

when he progressed. In your third-year lecture
I discussed his options after further treatment failure.

The one remaining option with some possibility
of benefit was bone marrow transplant. The mortality

from the treatment
(perhaps 20 percent) was equivalent

to the chance of cure. The transplant
program was previously funded by a grant,

which expired. We then discovered
that the hospital cost of $100,000 was not covered

by insurance. Intensive chemo and G-CSF to stimulate
white-cell recovery was estimated

to cost $7,000 per course and was denied
for outpatient or home care. We applied

for outside support
since his family members purportedly

had no funds. Four years of schooling
and perhaps five more years of grueling

training is reduced to this
single patient crisis.

What you do
when P. R. comes to you

will determine
your next forty or fifty years in medicine.